Make It Shine

Cultural and Inspirational Poetry

by Ingrid Dover-Vidal

First Printed in United Kingdom 2017

Published by Conscious Dreams Publishing
www.consciousdreamspublishing.com

Printed by: Ingramspark

ISBN 978-1-9998091-6-4

To Nicol

Thanks for all your support.
Enjoy the Journey!

F. P. Bover- Vidal

3.7.21

Dedication

To the memory of my parents, Samuel Prince Albert Dover, Senior and Susan Evelyn Dover, who created a little spark and lit my linguistic fire.

For my brothers; Raymond, Joseph, Lindon, Patrick, Sammy-D, Stephen and sister Diane.

And to the next generation... invest in your spirituality and culture to achieve even greater things than these.

Acknowledgements

Firstly, I would like to thank God for the strength and motivation to see my dream of becoming a published writer become a reality. I would like to thank everyone who has encouraged me to write and has given me opportunities to perform, entertain and stimulate others through my poetic voices.

I want to thank all my teachers who spurred me on with my writing in the early days in Ladbroke Grove. I especially want to thank Mr Goodwin from Bevington Primary School. He is also the author of the book 'There Ain't No Angels No More'. I would like to thank my High School English teacher Mr Neil Fee, who often wrote 'thought-provoking' on my work, which inspired me no end!

Gratitude also goes out to The English and Media Centre, Pimlico, for organising a crazy Creative Writing weekend to Celmi, Wales, for new teachers. This gave birth to some of my early nature-inspired poetry in 1984.

I pay tribute to the *African Caribbean Educational Research* project, (ACER) spearheaded in the early 80's by Len Garrison, who ran an annual *Black Penmanship Awards* competition. This allowed my work to reach more people and, in turn, allowed me to encourage this cultural focus amongst my students who also took their writing to a wider audience.

Thanks also to supportive staff and to the many students who I was fortunate enough to teach or mentor at Parliament Hill, Preston Manor, Canons High School and Loreto College, St Albans. Thanks to Keven, Nidhi, Albania, Adele, Nicola and cousins

Carol and Michelle, for encouraging me to share my poetry in assemblies and more widely in the community.

Special thanks to my faithful crowd of encouragers: Kemi, Marilyn, Beverley, Angela, Bimbola, Dayo, Sue, Patsy, Mary, Michelle and the Patterson family. Love and gratitude to my two guiding stars Novlette Bennett and Marcelle Roujade, whose timely introductions, just a few months ago, led to this whirlwind of my publishing journey. I thank you so much!

Nuff nuff thanks to all my family and friends on Facebook who have encouraged me to keep going. I am grateful to my online Writing Community W.R.I.T.E (Women Remain Inspired To Elevate), led by author and Book Journey Mentor Daniella Blechner, with much-valued expertise from Live Streaming Mentor Janine Cummings, who have enabled me to launch myself more visibly as a published poet.

Thanks again to Daniella for not only editing but also for her lead in bringing the anthology to publication with Conscious Dreams Publishing. I'm also grateful to her supportive, hands-on technical crew especially Nadia Vitushynska for typesetting and giving the cover that extra flair. Thank you to Rhoda Molife for providing an extra pair of eyes in the preparation of my biography.

To my family of believers who have helped to sustain my faith and vision through challenging and victorious times... don't ever stop!

And finally, thanks so much to my beloved Noel, Jelani and Lily for all their support and encouragement on my poetic journey.

Contents

Introduction

Having taught in London Schools for over three decades, my love of teaching and planting seeds of knowledge and understanding into the young minds of tomorrow has always given me great joy and much satisfaction. The writing of *Make It Shine!* has enabled me to play my part in helping to move them on to the next level. This has borne much fruit, not solely in terms of academic success, but also in terms of helping to reconnect so many of our young people who lacked the motivation to cherish education, by having higher but realistic aspirations for themselves, beyond the limited expectations of many of their peers.

My love of words, rhythms, Caribbean dialects and poetic forms, coupled with my love of bringing the characters and ideas alive through performance, have also been a driving force on my journey as a writer. This journey began having been inspired by my mother in her quest to build the cultural gap between Guyana and England. She accomplished this through sharing letters from my maternal Grandma and my aunts back home as well as through sharing memories of school days, folk songs, tales, parenting, proverbs and events which developed a patriotic pride and a sense of belonging. This is reflected in my poetry. The pursuit of happiness and fulfilment of a dream in a strange and foreign land is also paid tribute to in For Daddy: following in his steps. It is in passing the cultural baton on to future generations, through some of the oral traditions of Guyana, the Caribbean and Africa and by spurring youngsters on, (especially those who lack the cultural connections to the positive achievements of our ancestors which preceded the trans-Atlantic slave trade) that I intend to inspire others to shine.

By reaching out to the young people with my performance poetry, I intend to engage their attention and stimulate their enthusiasm for developing a greater sense of their historical achievements and to widen their vision for all they can become. I believe that in sharing my personal story of perseverance and by paying tribute to our past and modern-day heroes and heroines, that students both young and old will pursue their dreams and desires with greater clarity. I hope that my work will not only succeed in raising the self-esteem of individuals from African and Caribbean backgrounds but will help to promote a greater universal appreciation for the achievements within these communities and beyond. My goal is to enable them to celebrate their past and embrace current opportunities for personal, spiritual and cultural growth as well as to encourage self-expression using a variety of poetic mediums.

Cultural / Spiritual Identity

Beginnings: Part One

Slavery done but still not free?
Why do these chains still hinder me?
Slavery done but still not free?
Come, let us learn from History
Help me trace my ancestry

Mother Africa
Gave birth to me
Nursed and cared for the whole family
Carved out great
Civilizations
Empires flourished
And many nations

From a continent of peoples
not content
to sit back and wait with a begging bowl
to make them whole
our people had
SOUL
SPIRIT
And STRENGTH of mind
To chisel out treasures of many kinds.

Between 400 BC and 100 AD
First African converts to Christianity
From north eastern African shores
The Axumite Empire was born
Also known then as Ethiopia
Famous as a trading nation

Home of the Royal Queen of Sheba
People of wealth, faith and great vision meant
They could accomplish great things
Wherever they went.

Moving forward to medieval days
Nigeria boasts the city of Benin;
Like the Great Wall of China,
Its city walls stood staunch
Proud and defensive on every side.

Wise women led the way in the battle plans
Queen Candace of Meroe defeated
A Macedonian man —
Alexander the Great around 300 BC
From her military brilliance
He was forced to withdraw
And mount his campaign at Egypt's door.

So, grow where you're planted
And cherish every seed
Nurture it with knowledge
Of our great ancestry
Let slavery be done
And freedom reign
Renewed by our past
We can make it past the pain.
Make it past the pain.
Make it past the pain.

Part Two

"So since
We are surrounded
By such a great
CROWN
Of witnesses"*

Let us
With perseverance run
Run the race etched out for us*
Moulding
Shaping
Chiselling
Creating
As we journey
Giving nothing but our best

Make
Mother Africa's
Tears of Joy
Pour forth like a mountain spring
Refreshing every orifice
Of her being

Prodigal sons and daughters
Return to embrace the truth
Having traced the roots
Of our African Beginnings

---

* Inspired by Hebrews12:1(NIV)

Spurred on by Ancestral voices
Of Victorious Nubian Princes and Princesses
Let us no longer linger
Languishing over past hurts and atrocities
Acknowledge the pangs of slavery
And phoenix-like
Fuelled by our faith
Let us ascend to higher heights
and
   Submerge
      to deeper depths
         of self-fulfilment

Like our first Century brothers and sisters,
Let us together build with precious gems
Upon their strong foundation
Of knowledge
Skills and Arts
And take our rightful place as
Worthy contributors to World Civilisation

Let us not with this new-found knowledge
Be bellowed into pompous pride
To don the mantle of the expert
But like a good measure
Shaken-up and evenly laid
We may become what many crave
And live to make a difference.

Unchained

No longer shackled by African roots in slavery
Our roots go much deeper
They penetrate through centuries of
Architectural excellence
Benin City calls out to me
Its walls surround and protect me
Its people traded successfully on
her West African shores

The spirit lifts me
And gives life
New sight
A vision to embrace
Propel your thoughts
To reach new heights
Limit not yourself to
Historical misconceptions
Seek after evidence that demands a verdict
You be the judge
And live.

Fusion

The bell's been rung
But still not free?
It is my God who LIBERATES me

Misconceptions of God rule this city
Is he black, is he white, brown or Chinese?
But all this mix up is not necessary
For the Word clearly states that God is spirit, you see
And it is my God who LIBERATES me

Deep penetrating spirit
Burning from within
Breaks the yoke of bondage;
Captivity to sin

Equal opportunity
And still not free,
It is my God who LIBERATES me.

Some of us have found a brand-new slavery
To work from Sunday to Sunday for more money
But we make a mistake if we think that will set us free
It is my God who LIBERATES me.

I won't be tied to my job or to my P.C.
Or insulate my conscience with what's best or cosy
For at the break of day it will be clear to see
It is my God who LIBERATES me.

Be all that you can be: a universal message
But not if it means stepping over others,
My sisters, my brothers you're still not free —
It is my God who LIBERATES me.

A new creation! And purpose too.
Go win the world for Christ is what He said I must do
Stop sighing and prolonging the agony,
For where the Spirit of the Lord is there is
LIBERTY,
LIBERTY,
LIBERTY!

Why don't you find out why He paid the price?
So you can live a life of self-sacrifice.
Giving, but never giving up,
Moving, but with a forward thrust.

In CHRIST you can have VICTORY!
He can do it for you;
For He has truly *LIBERATED ME!*

(1989)

Delight

Like this candle which stands here lit
Help me to stand firm
Rooted and grounded in your word.
Secure in your unconditional love for me.

You are the glass jar that protects me
You harness the warmth and light
From the central glow
Reminding me of your presence
That ancient Spirit which lives within
Through rebirth

Though my flame may saunter from side to side,
Sometimes bent so low by passing breezes,
Still let me illuminate those around
Reflecting your goodness,
your Grace,
Your fragrance.

Though my wax be somewhat melted
The impressions I leave behind, from ledge to ledge
Reveal a Bayeux Tapestry,
A life of purpose planned and battled through
Yet existence continues;
Fuelled to the very centre of my wick;
Myself renewed.

Then let us not of oxygen be starved
By the untimely closing of a lid
But maintain the life within,

Fan into flame even the
Smallest
Flicker
Giving Hope
Giving breath,
giving life
to our dreams and purpose to our steps
rekindling within others
once more
the power to shine.

Adoption

I was birthed by Mother Africa
But quickly removed from her warm
Safe womb
To continue life on Caribbean shores

Of Ghanaian descent
They told me
Reflected in the people who came
The land of Guyana
My parents' country I took to my heart
Patriotic from the start
I had my flag, map and national song
Eldorado city cheered me along

The desire to achieve
My parents instilled in me
They worked hard for little money
But they built on the
Foundations of our ancestry
Africa not England, 'the mother country'
Africa not England, 'the mother country'

As I have grown,
I've learnt to absorb
The good of the past and
Lay the rest to waste
For many hurts
Can slow the heart down
Can make it bleed
Can bring a frown

Amazed by our 'little-known' History
Descended of kings and queens
Who me?
Yes! Many facts and artifacts too
Well you know what a little knowledge can do!

So, make it your business to read for yourself
And get a conviction to help you excel
May the limits to your success
Not be self-inflicted
As you grow in knowledge
And help expand your mind
May you see your Blackness differently,
Of the positive kind.

Fashion Me a People

Fashion me a people
Rhyme me a rhyme
Reveal to me a history
Back in time

Fashion me a people
Rhyme me a rhyme
Reveal to me a history
That should be mine

Tell of great achievers
Who battled to be free
Surmounted obstacles
To be the best that they could be

Nelson Mandela, we know so well
But what of Rosa Parks?
Arthur Wharton?
Charlotte Ray?

Fashion me a people
Rhyme me a rhyme
Reveal to me a history
Back in time

Who was the black inventor
Who gave us traffic lights?
Or the first black woman
Whoever took flight?

Tell of many triumphs
Won on the battlefield
Of the black regiments
Who refused yield.

Fashion me a people
Rhyme me a rhyme
Reveal to me a history
Back in time.

Let us be an inspiration
Let us take you on a tour
And with the key of knowledge
Open some closed doors

Fashion me a people
Rhyme me a rhyme
Reveal to me a history
Back in time

Fashion me a people
Rhyme me a rhyme
Reveal heroines and heroes
Who should be mine.

(2005)

Perseverance, Resilience & Renewal

Conviction in Action

When something touches us
We feel
We think
We examine
We decide and determine.

Often it ends just there
But I know and you really know
It is not enough.

Out of conviction
We speak
We act
We aren't just moved
We do move
Forward
We progress
We ignite and inspire
Fully activated by the spirit which spurs us on
We WILL do great things.

(1987)

You!

You are the wind beneath my wings
You are the purpose to my steps
You are the sound that I must sing
When other refrains seem to end.

You are the door beyond the bend
That leads to tomorrow's hope
You are the smile that lets me know
The journey's far from over yet.

(21/9/03)

Pride

Proud man
Sits on his Mountain Top
So high up
He thinks being proud will make him happy;
But it will not.

Proud man in need on his Mountain Top
Poor man trying to lend a hand
But pride steps in.
Proud man cannot accept his offer;
Shuts off instead.

Too high up to come down;
Down to humility and reality
You've got to humble yourself to be free;
Realise who you are,
Where you're going.

Proud man,
Throw away that extra pride
That stumbling block
Behind which you hide.

Leave your sun-scorched pride on the mountain top
And rise with new dignity.

Humble, humble like me
Humble, humble like he
Humble, humble like she
Humble, humble like WE!

All That Glitters

'All that glitters is not gold';
That's what mum would say when I was still at home.
The nights I stayed in when I wanted to rave,
Ignored her warnings;
Came back late.
But I didn't care;
I had my guy.

But even then,
I used to think of no-one but myself.
I began to blame them when things went wrong,
When they weren't there
To hold me,
To care for me,
To feed me.

I began to hate his friends, my friends, even Cath.
And where were Mum and Dad?
Mum didn't seem to want to know
And Dad couldn't help.

And him,
He's gone too.
All the glitter had worn off
And underneath…
It wasn't even silver;
Just a faded kind of bronze.

So, there I was;
Just me,
Left
In a room with a child,
Surrounded by people who I thought should help,
Who seemed bereft of feeling
But what could I do?
'Think positive!' I was told;
'Only you can help yourself now.'
'You've got to humble yourself to be free;
Realise who you are, where you're headed'
'Take what you've got and build on it.'

Well I've got something and she's mine.
I've found new pride
And with it we'll step forward;
Together we'll make our Gold.

(1980)

Waiting

Time slips slowly by
As I try
To fathom the depths of God's love for me
That allows me to endure
Delay,
After
Delay
After
Delay;
Each one
A temporary pain,
Purposefully placed
Compelling me to tighten my
Grip on the spiritual reality
With which he's
Moulding me
Shaping me
Until he produces in me
That little something
To sustain me,
To remind me of his glory
And place
His word
Or a song
In my heart
To encourage others.

"Bwoy, he mus' love me bad!"

(24/10/03)

A Changing Appetite

Life is full of mixed transition
From the cradle to the grave
And through every challenge
We pray that we can be brave

If we're blessed or just lucky
There's someone to lead us on
To take the next step
Make the decision
To move our life along.

But gradually we move from trust
To
Insecurity
One teacher leaves,
Then another
'what is to become of me?'
The dependence that has grown
has left me all lopsided
'On whom shall I lean now
that my confidence's subsided?'

I have skills I can apply
But I need to top them up.
Right now,
I just can't fly
For I feel like
I would

DROP!

But I sure as won't give up
I'll find out what I need to do
To help me drink now of this cup
Till my success comes shining through!

Legacy

Don't let anybody
Wind you up
Control your emotions
Spin you like a top
Take hold of the reigns of self-control
Or you may go too far
And find you can't stop.

Focus your mind on who you are
The journey you're on and
Where you're coming from

Remember your parents' hopes for you;
There's nothing they wouldn't do
To see you through.
Your mentors can only
Spur you on;
Give direction.

But it's Your song
That shall be sung.

Will it be a sweet refrain
If the work's not done?
Or a deadly dirge in mourning?
Half a page in remembrance…

When you've gone from here —
Don't tell me that you just don't care,
For in your heart of hearts
I sense much fear

About the years ahead;
When you should be soaring
You'll sink like lead
Well below what you can do.
In the law of averages — just think about it
The elevation's up to you.

Transitions

Every change is a loss;
A reason for grieving?
I look to the Cross,
The fall of man:
A change from innocence
To knowing
Adam and Eve
grieved.

But some changes bring joy
Of being set free
Now surrounded by unfamiliarity
A new insecurity gives birth
To trust
As we take hold of our
New position
We must
let go of all that binds us
To failings of the past
No longer heed their summons
But rather fix our hearts
On the bonding that lasts.

Give healing its time;
Let it run its course
Renewed and replenished
Grateful for the source.

(31/08/02)

Attitude Is Everything

A woman without hope gives up
Is wiped out.
The hopeful woman
Is encouraged by a victorious end
Her decision enacted
    She goes on and
is renewed.

(1987)

Bullying

It Na Funny

It na funny
It na funny

When you feel to gimme licks
It na funny
So yu could have you little KICKS
It na funny
When yu stalk me like your prey
It na funny
When de pain won't go away.

It na funny
It na funny

When yu hol' me 'gainst de wall
It na funny
When yu stan' an' watch me bawl
It na funny
When no one came to my defence
It na funny
When dem said it was nonsense

It na funny
It na funny

When I start to hol' me HEAD
When me blood, it did run RED
I did wish dat I was
DEAD!

AN DAT NA FUNNY
NO,
DAT NA FUNNY.

Not My Business...

Have you ever seen or heard
Someone being bullied
And never said a word?

Turned a blind eye,
Or looked the other way
Frozen by fear of
What the BULLY might say?
The BULLY might say?
the BULLY might say?

Why don't you answer the question?
And tell me no lie,
was it you I just saw passing by
with your conscience closed
Your excuse ready?
To protect yourself
Hold your alibi steady!

'But you don't understand
She's bigger than me
And muscles like that don't grow on no tree'.

I've been a victim;
It wasn't pleasant
In fact, she left me
with quite a present
Of cuts and
    bruises and
        Dirty looks
            I

couldn't concentrate
On my books

I couldn't grass
I couldn't tell
Transfixed by terror;
A living hell.

So now you know why I
Stand by
I still have scars
Sometimes they
CRY.

Love
&
Romance

Forever True

Promises are forever
Never let them fade away
Dreams are for pursuing
Don't let a thing stand in your way;

Nothing present
Nothing past,
We need a love
that's gonna last.

A love that leaves me feeling warm;
Security amidst the storms
A love embrace;
A reassuming smile
A sincere openness
That stands out a mile.

Let tarnished habits flee,
No longer stay
Ignite affection
Let's stand
Inspired by each other's love
Always.

(14/2/95)

My Valentine

My valentine wears red
Beneath his
Bronzed
Jamaican
Complexion;
His blood
Runs freely
Along well travelled veins
Pulsating motions move his heart
Closer to mine
Our eyes meet
Heart beats synchronize
In the timely embrace
Two become one.

(14/2/97)

Poetic
Rhythms

De Shoppin'

You hear you modda a call you
As you lal-loff in you bed:
'Shawn! Get up!
Come do de shoppin'
Before me box you in you 'ead!'

You get up, fling on a pants an' ting
Before she slippa reach.
Bwoy, you don't want to vex you Modda
Before she start to preach!

You hustle down de stairs
An' straight to de kitchen you gawn
But you han' get ketch in de dumpling bowl
As you Modda halla :
"Shawn, You tidy you bedroom yet?"
"Yes, Maam.
"You empty de cat litter tray?"
"You brush up you teet' dem CLEAN, CLEAN,
CLEAN,
An you pack di dishes away?"
"Maam!"

"For me not able take no shame
down a' Wembley Market fi you,
Dis bright an' breezy Saturday mornin'
I have nuff t'ings to do!"

At last you both get out de house
And who is it you meet?
Sista Mary from de Baptist Church
An' her daughter Louise look sweet!
"Good morning, Sister Mary."
"God bless your soul today."
"But wait; is that you little son Shawn?
What a way him grow big, eeeeh!"

"Is de dumplin' dem I give him
An' de ackee an' sal' fish too.
"An' how he love me fry plantain
wid a little callaloo stew."

"Will we be seeing you in Church tomorrow?
Pastor putting on a big do.
For all de Missing in Action
Don't t'ink I talking 'bout you."

"Well de Lord knows my situation
I meet wid him every day.
Plus me na able with de four hours
Unu like to stay there an' pray!"

"Everyone have a different calling, Miss Carol.
So I say to each his own.
But please tell your son
Tek he eye off me daughter
Tell him leave me chil' alone.

"Mummy he never trouble me.
He just trying a friendly t'ing."
"Girl, little beginnings have great endings —
You don't know what bwoy pickney bring!"

"What start with a look
Could make you fling way de book
Kiss you teet' to study and ting.
It's a little early to become a Mummy
And dat without wedding ring!"

"Don't worry 'bout dat,
My Shawn is de tops:
Born to do great things
Like get a degree from University
And become a big somebody!"

Hear Shawn now: "life is my university,
That's where I'll get my first-class degree
Watch me, just wait and see."

With all this empty boasting done
Miss Carol watch her rough-neck son
As her head did swell with pride
Miss Mary shout, "Have you applied?"

Well you thought that was fighting talk
So straight away you hail de bus
You coax your modda on it
Before she start to cuss.

You finally finish de shopping
And glad to phone a friend
Cos you know there's no more shopping
Till Saturday come again.

And just to think Modda did warn You
Not to bring Her no disgrace
And is you hustle Her away
To save a bit of face!

So, remember, when you meet up with a long-lost
Sister
play it cool that you will leave there
without even a blister!

(2005)

Music

MUSIC
MUSIC
MUSIC
Ca me sey MUSIC!

The music of the birds
The music of the trees
The rhythm of the stream has captured me.

Me sey me strapped to de seat
By a musical beat
Of de water racing to catch up to de sea.

You may t'ink it na mek sense
Dat dis feelin' dat I sense
Is so intense
Because de water it a rush
As if it mus' catch bus.

"Hush na, Water.
Why you mek so much noise?
Cool yourself; there's no need to hurry."

"De sheep dem did hurry,
An' look wha' happen'
Ain't they had was to leave
A piece a dem coat."

"So hush na, Water.
Why you mek so much noise?
Cool yourself; there's no need to worry."

"Take your time an' enjoy
de rippling,
de rolling,
de strolling
Over rocks
and stones
Moulded into shape
by a continuous source
Of vitality
That gives them life.
Refreshing to the eye,
To de ear
to de nose,
Even de hair a sway in de breeze;
It feels relief.

(1984)

Upon a Stile

Here I sit upon a stile;
A rest, a break in my journey.
A chance at last to take in,
To feel
To smell
To touch
To observe.

To look at the tangled wool
Caught on the barbed wire
Hanging in loops as if
Spun by a spinner
Secured to the wire which
Grips so tightly.

What a fight to release
Something so gentle,
So soft to touch,
So fresh and clean to smell;
It makes a pleasant feeling
To rest my hand in a pocket full.

Oh, how I envy the lambs
Snuggled up to their mums;
It's warm there.
In her they too find
Warmth,
Strength
Comfort:
A pleasant reassuring feeling

Like being cared for
Like being loved.

But I have pondered too long upon this seat
I now feel a hardness,
A numbness beneath me.
Yes, the strength has returned at last to my limbs.

Not far to go now.
That large stone ahead
Marks the end of my journey.

I must go and leave this sun-warmed seat
For 'another' weary traveller.

(1984)

Above the Clouds

Above the clouds that shadow my path,
On sunnier moments, days, we glide,
Suspended over the firmaments;
heaven like.

As we descend now,
Clouds like smog engulf us,
Give their final embrace and
Unwillingly release us
Into seas of blue, indigo,
and violet.

First the water reveals itself,
Then Land's End fills my view.
Bungalows become visible.

There is life here,
A sense of community,
Runway in sight
Touch down is gentle.

Welcome to Barbados!!!

(23/05/98)

Tributes

Shane

This morning, I woke up and smiled at the rain
I decide to write a poem
'bout a boy named Shane.

I coax him, remind him, again and again
To bring his books to lessons —
The boy is driving me insane!

I say, "Shane, when you're grown
What do you want to be?
A doctor, a mechanic or a person like me,

Who strives to do her best
When put to the test
Accepting every challenge;
Leave retreating to the rest."

"When you grow up, I want you to be proud
Of all your achievements,
Not how you hung around
Watching other students work
As you SKYLARK
Lickin' lyrics all day long
From dusk 'til dark"

"Hey, Miss. Check me,
I'm a wicked MC.
Just watch me go —
Watch my style,
Watch my flow!"

"Those things won't run away,
they will wait for you.
HEAD DOWN!
Hand UP!
Don't mind what others do.
Persevering every day
Will see you through.
For at the end of the day
SHANE,
It's up to you!

Tribute to Benji

It was Thursday de eighteenth
A little after noon
Benji Zephaniah did a step inna de room.

Nuff 9th Years did a gather
In de fiction library,
Not knowing fi true
What they really woulda see!

We had recently read
Some of his Dub wise poetry,
'bout how he really love he "mudda"
And "set Mandela free!"

He achieved very little
When he was a yout'
He did not love his school days,
If you want to know the truth!'.

But now he use he talent
To talk 'bout History;
Past and present happenings —
No longer a mystery.

We got encouragement to
Write down our thoughts too;
A poem, a story,
Create something new.

So, take these things to heart,
Whatever you do
Education is a tool —
Make it work for you!

A Verse for Bobby

Tall and majestic
She towers above her peers
A mellow complexion,
Streams of black curly hair.

Her image:
A picture of laughter and friendship
A caring nature,
Magnetic and true
Below it there broods
A lack of contentment
Basking in boredom
'There's nothing to do!'

A treasure of intellect
Untapped and buried
The key turns by her will,
Unlocking so much.
She's an unfinished symphony
Still in it's infancy;
A fire whose embers
Flicker at times.
"Bobby,
Only desire will
Rekindle the passion
Delight in possibilities
Make the future bright.

For only then will your
Heart feel accomplished
Compelled on by loved ones
Who have vision for you.
Although they may chide you
And you feel like
Rebelling
Be true to your talents
Let the real you shine through.

(2002)

To Our Son

You are a credit to your parents
You are the apple of their eye
You are the promise that Sir gave you;
'If you want to, you can fly!'
You can soar above the clouds
You can see the vision through
Whatever you accomplish
it's up to God
and up to you.
So, don't be limited by the past;
You aim straight
You aim high
and with a steady pull
you just watch those arrows fly!
You may not always hit your target
or rejoice with a bulls-eye
but as your quiver's full
keep at it;
have another try.
Apply all that you are learning
be inquisitive —
keep yearning.
Be the best that you can be
GO THE DISTANCE
and be free from nagging doubts and fears
that could cripple you for years.
Unleash that mighty, un-tapped power.
Be blessed
Be bold
and seize the hour!

Tribute to a Black Mother

It's mother's birthday again;
I want to buy a card,
One that truly conveys
My feelings for my Black Mother.
Not the type which hits you
Like sweetly scented flowers,
Or like make-up, smooths,
Every blemish covered
Leaving it impersonal,
A ghostly negative.

But is there such a card?

O Mother,
To reach inside your mind, your thoughts
To let you know how much we love you,
We, your children:
Heirs to your love and devotion
Inheritors of a rich History
As yet but half discovered.

To have known you, is to have known love,
To have shared love, is to care.
For, Black love exhibited
cannot be limited;
Its flow is infinite
It's always there.

In you there lies that inner strength
Developed by our female progenitors
Kindled during slavery;
The fire burns on.

You surmount the pressures of today
Increased by those who scorn
Our Blackness,
Our Beauty,
Which become in us a source of pride;
You stand pompous nor vain
But dignified.

Poised to discern every situation,
With maternal wisdom,
you thoughtfully guide me.
Instilled in my youth, your proverbs still echo
Tones of approval and disapproval.
When pushed to the limit with comfort I recall:
'De hotta de battle, de sweeta de victory'
'when you han' in lion mout', pat 'e head!'
I am forewarned, forearmed;
I am aware, I am prepared.

I am constantly exhorted to aim high
In failure, I want to try again
Without fear or obligation to anyone but myself.
Fuelled by your faith
You dispel my anxieties
You cherish my hopes
I too am renewed.

All this you give
All this you are.

Is there such a card whose covers
can contain such sentiments?

Now that the question lies redundant in my
          consciousness
Let these words
Dear Mother,
Serve as a token
Of your immeasurable worth.

(1985)

For Daddy: Following in His Steps

When Samuel sailed to England back in April 1960,
Who thought that he would still be here in 1982!
The vessel that he boarded left from Port of Spain,
Hailed as the T.N. Montserrat,
people hardly went by plane.

Before reaching Southampton
They docked at many an Isle,
Hopefuls piled on from Barbados, St Kitts, Grenada
          and Antigua
The food in Spain did not compare;
Not many people smiled.

We came from lands of sunshine
Where the cold wind did not blow,
To a land of milk and honey;
At least they told us so.

We battled seas of racism
As we settled in.
Determined to get somewhere
Determined we would win
The respect of our people
Who had come here years before.
We were not seeking charity
We worked harder —
All the more.

Dad sacrificed a lot of things to make the journey here,
He studied hard and sweated to build up a good career.
Eyes focused on the place back home
　　　his children could inherit,
He taught us how to save and for ourselves gain merit.

Now, as you face the future
　　　with a rich history behind
Build a strong foundation
　　　that will help expand your mind.
Your freedom lies within yourself;
You better had believe it,
Don't waste a minute or an hour
Take hold of it
Invest that power!

(13/10/03)

In Praise of Learning

School's out for summer; take off the uniform
A brand-new independence, no longer time to mourn
For school day friends who we will miss
More than French and Arithmetic.

For fond farewells sealed with a kiss
And favourite teachers; 'Yes, Sir', 'Please, Miss!'
They worked so hard to help me see
My dream become a reality.

As I reflect on lessons learned
On knowledge gained and merits earned
Let me not squander all I've got;
Grasp opportunities, seize the lot.

The clock of learning never stops
But signals new openings
New challenges
New plots.

When faced with disappointment
With courage,
Do press on.
May you know the joy of reaching goals
That move your life along.

As this hour closes
May another soon begin
And whichever path you choose
Be determined,
You can win.

(June 1998)

About the Author

Ingrid Dover-Vidal was born in Georgetown, Guyana. She came to England in the early 1960s and grew up in Ladbroke Grove in west London. After secondary school, she trained as a teacher of English and Drama, going on to teach these subjects as well as Religious Education and various learning development intervention courses in a teaching career spanning 34 years.

Ingrid has written, produced and directed several plays and written many short stories and poems. Her poetry encompasses a variety of themes such as love, bullying and resilience. She cites her influences as the US poets Maya Angelou and Marie Evans, the Jamaican poets Valerie Bloom and Benjamin Zephaniah, the Guyanese poets Grace Nichols and John Agard and English poets such as Wordsworth and Gerald Manley-Hopkins.

Her poetic pathway reflects the seeds of her faith, family life and delight in her discovery and appreciation of Black History. Ingrid's desire is to first and foremost utilise her love of language and cultural rhythms to help improve students' self-esteem. She strives to encourage their creativity and promote the untapped potential of the young minds that she entertains and inspires in both the classroom and the wider community.

This anthology of poetry also reflects the influence of her father Samuel's penchant for diary entries. *Pride* clearly reflects on events and experiences as seen through the eyes of a 15-year-old teenager; later, the more mature voice of spiritual and cultural awareness can be heard in *Beginnings* and *Unchained*. She ends the anthology with poetic tributes honouring past students and acknowledging the foundations our elders laid for us to build upon.

Today, Ingrid continues to teach on a part-time basis and incorporates her writings as well as performances of poetry and Caribbean folk songs into her lessons.

Lightning Source UK Ltd.
Milton Keynes UK
UKHW021329040619

343840UK00006B/505/P

9 781999 809164